AMERICA IS BORN
(1770–1800)

TITLE LIST

AMERICA IS BORN
(1770-1800)

WITHDRAWN

BY CONSTANCE SHARP

MASON CREST

Mason Crest
370 Reed Road
Broomall, Pennsylvania 19008
www.masoncrest.com

Printed and bound in Hashemite Kingdom of Jordan.

First printing
9 8 7 6 5 4 3 2 1

Library of Congress Cataloging-in-Publication Data

Sharp, Constance.
   America is born, 1770-1800 / by Constance Sharp.
      p. cm. — (How America became America)
   Includes index.
   ISBN 978-1-4222-2399-4 (hardcover) — ISBN 978-1-4222-2396-3 (hardcover series) ISBN 978-1-4222-9309-6 (ebook)
 1. United States—Politics and government—1775-1783—Juvenile literature. 2. United States—Politics and government—1783-1809—Juvenile literature. I. Title.
   E302.1.S53 2012
   973.3—dc22
                              2011000839

Produced by Harding House Publishing Services, Inc.
www.hardinghousepages.com
Cover design by Torque Advertising + Design.

1765–Parliament passes the Stamp Act. Riots break out across the American colonies.

October 1765–Delegates from nine colonies meet in New York City at the Stamp Act Congress.

1774–Parliament responds to the Boston Tea Party with the Intolerable Acts.

September 1774–The First Continental Congress meets in Philadelphia.

April 18, 1775–Paul Revere rides from Boston to wake up the Minutemen, shouting news of the British march toward Lexington and Concord. The first battles of the American Revolution begin the next day.

January 1776–Thomas Paine writes a book called Common Sense. It calls for America to declare independence from Britain.

March 17, 1766–Parliament takes back the Stamp Act, but passes the Declaratory Act.

March 5, 1770–A clash between a small group of British soldiers and a mob of angry townspeople leads to the Boston Massacre.

May 1773–Parliament passes the Tea Act. This gives the British East India Company total control over all tea coming to the colonies. It also makes the tea tax lower for them.

December 16, 1773–Colonists fight against the Tea Act with the Boston Tea Party.

July 4, 1776–The Continental Congress agrees to sign the Declaration of Independence.

May 10, 1775–The Second Continental Congress gets together. They decide to create a Continental Army and make George Washington its leader.

June 17, 1775–The Battle of Bunker Hill.

May 25, 1787–The Constitutional Convention gets together in Philadelphia to write a new Constitution. They show it to the delegates on September 17.

1794–The Whiskey Rebellion begins in western Pennsylvania. George Washington leads the army to put an end to the law breaking. This shows the power of the central government.

September 3, 1783–The United States and Britain sign the Treaty of Paris, ending the Revolutionary War. Britain agrees to treat the United States as an independent country.

1787–Congress passes the Northwest Ordinance. This describes how new states will join the Union. All new states will have the same rights as old states.

1800–President Adams goes to the Convention of 1800 with France. This ends all fighting between the two countries.

November 15, 1777–The Continental Congress says yes to the Articles of Confederation. This is an early version of the Constitution.

February 4, 1789–The first presidential election is held. Everyone votes for George Washington, who becomes president, with John Adams as his Vice President.

1791–Congress approves the Bill of Rights, the first ten changes to the Constitution.

July 14, 1798–Congress passes the Alien and Sedition Acts. This makes it harder to become an American citizen. It also made it a crime to write bad and untrue things about the government.

March 4, 1789–The new United States Constitution becomes law.

1797–Washington's time as president ends. John Adams becomes the second president, with Thomas Jefferson as his Vice President.

The TIMES are Dreadful Doleful Dismal Dolorous, and DOLLAR-LESS.

of the STAN

An Emblem of the Effects of the fatal Stamp

Thursday, *October 31. 1765*

NUMB 1195

THE PENNSYLVANIA JOURNAL;
AND
WEEKLY ADVERTISER.

EXPIRING: In Hopes of a Refurrection to LIFE again.

I am forry to be obliged to acquaint my readers that as the Stamp Act is feared to be obligatory upon us after the *firſt of November* enfuing (The Fatal To-morrow), The publiſher of this paper, unable to bear the Burthen, has thought it expedient to ſtop a while, in order to deliberate, whether any methods can be found to elude the chains forged for us, and eſcape the infupportable flavery, which it is hoped, from the laſt repreſentation now made againſt that act, may be effected. Mean while I muſt earneſtly Requeſt every individual of my Subſcribers, many of whom have been long behind Hand, that they would immediately diſcharge their reſpective Arrears, that I may be able, not only to ſupport myſelf during the Interval, but be better prepared to proceed again with this Paper whenever an opening for that purpoſe appears, which I hope will be ſoon.

WILLIAM BRADFORD.

A newspaper account of the Tax Act protest.

Chapter 1
TAXING THE COLONIES

In 1765, more than one and a half million people lived in the **American colonies**. For the past hundred and fifty years, people had been coming to the colonies from Great Britain and other parts of Europe. Towns and cities had grown up. The land had become more settled. That didn't mean life was always easy, though. For many of the **colonists**, especially those away from the cities, making a home and finding food still meant lots of hard work.

The people who came to the American colonies needed to be brave. The land changed the people. They weren't the same people as they had been before they got there. They were different from the people they had had been when they lived in Europe.

Still, the colonists thought of themselves as British. And Britain thought of them as British citizens. Britain had planted colonies all over the world. The colonies made money

Colonies are groups of people living in a land outside of their original country. They still have to take orders from the government of their homeland.

Colonists are people who live in colonies.

for Britain. They helped make Britain stronger. As long as the American colonies sent money back to Britain and helped out whenever there was a war, the British government was happy.

Slowly, though, the colonists were becoming Americans. They had a lot more in common with each other than with the people back in Britain. They no longer thought of themselves as British.

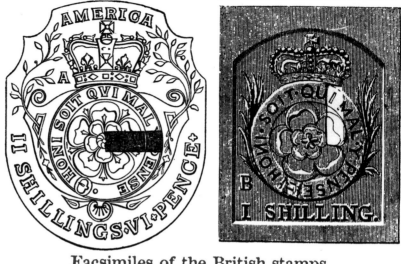

Facsimiles of the British stamps

When the British **Parliament** passed the Stamp Act, Britain expected the colonists to go along with it without much fuss. The Stamp Act was a way for Britain to get more money from their American colonies. Britain had just fought a long war with France, Spain, and other countries. Parliament thought the American colonies should help pay for the war.

The Stamp Act put a **tax** on almost every kind of paper. All papers used in legal documents. All licenses. Even calendars, newspapers, and playing cards would be taxed.

Parliament is a group of British leaders who make up one part of the government.

A **tax** is extra money owed to the government on top of the normal price.

To show how angry they were, sometimes the colonists hung clothes stuffed to look like a British member of Parliament.

The American colonists were angry about the new taxes. Nobody had even asked them what they thought. Nobody was speaking up for them in the British Parliament.

They colonists thought they paid Britain enough taxes already. Plus, they paid taxes to their own colonies' governments. Now this! It was just too much.

Britain found people living in the colonies to act as "stamp masters." These men would collect the new tax and send it back to Britain. The other colonists were angry that these men had agreed to collect the tax. They called the men traitors. So most stamp masters quit their new jobs. They realized they had to choose between being American and being British.

Men from many of the colonies met in New York City. They wrote up a **Declaration** of **Rights** to send to the British king and Parliament. They were loyal to Britain, they wrote, but they thought they should be equal to other British citizens. They wanted someone to stand up for them in British Parliament. They wanted someone to make sure they were treated fairly.

When someone says something clearly, and in public, they are making a **declaration**.

A person's **rights** are the things she is owed, and can expect to receive.

The colonists refused to have anything to do with the Stamp Act. They stopped doing business with Britain. They didn't want to use the stamps.

Finally, the British Parliament gave up on the Stamp Act. They weren't happy about it, though. They didn't like the colonies telling them what to do.

The next year, Parliament passed another law. This one was called the Townsend Acts. It was a set of new taxes. Britain still wanted to make sure it was getting all the money it could from its colonies. The British government also wanted to make sure the colonists knew who was in charge. The new taxes were on things like glass, paper, paint, and tea.

Editorial cartoon about the repeal of the Stamp Act

The colonists were angry again. They refused to go along with this new tax either. Most of them stopped buying these things from the British. They either made their own or did without. Sometimes, they smuggled things down from Canada.

Eventually, Parliament gave up on all the taxes except for the tax on tea. The colonists were drinking smuggled tea so they didn't care. Then, in 1773, the British Parliament passed the Tea Act. The Tea Act said that only one company could sell tea in the colonies. It also lowered the tea tax. This meant that British **merchants** could now sell tea cheaper than the smugglers could.

Britain thought the colonists would be happy their tea was cheaper. Instead, the colonists were angry. They still didn't want to be taxed without having someone in Parliament speaking on their behalf.

In cities along the coast, ships filled with tea arrived from Britain. In some cities, the colonists wouldn't let the ships dock. In others, they unloaded the tea, but they locked it up in warehouses. Then they left it to rot.

Then, three ships filled with tea docked in Boston. The colonists were furious. They had a meeting and made a plan. A group of men dressed up like Natives and swarmed the docks. They jumped onto the ships and dumped all the tea in the harbor.

The Boston Tea Party, as the **riot** became known, made the British Parliament mad. They decided to punish the American colonists. So Parliament quickly passed another series of acts. The acts were supposed to get the American colonies under control.

Merchants are business people who buy, sell, and trade things.

A **riot** happens when a big group of people gets violent and starts destroying things.

The new acts were worse than anything Parliament had done yet. The colonists called them the Intolerable Acts. (If something is intolerable, you simply can't stand it!)

One of the Intolerable Acts closed down Boston Harbor until the colonists paid for all the tea they had dumped in the harbor. Another act gave the governor of Massachusetts the power to pick all the colonies' leaders. Town meetings were now against the law unless the governor gave his permission.

Now the colonists had even less control. They were angry and frustrated.

In 1774, people from all of the thirteen colonies met in Philadelphia. These men were called **delegates**. They still felt loyal to Britain, but they wanted better laws. The meeting was called the First Continental Congress.

King George III

The delegates wrote up the Declaration of Rights and **Grievances** and sent it to King George III. They wanted the king to listen to them. They wanted to be able to get along with Britain and work things out.

Some people, though, were starting to wonder if that was possible. Maybe, they wondered, it was time for the colonies to no longer be part of Britain.

Delegates are people chosen to speak on someone else's behalf. They stand up for the interests of the people who elected them.

Grievances are like complaints. They say what is wrong and what needs changing.

TOGETHER WE STAND!

Have you ever noticed that if you and someone else get mad about the same thing, you end up feeling closer to each other? Maybe a bunch of students think a teacher is being unfair. Or maybe you and your brother or sister are angry with your parents because they won't let you do something you both want to do. Or maybe you and another kid at school are upset with a bully who has been giving both of you a hard time. When something like that happens, you usually end up feeling closer to each other. Something about facing the same problem pulls people together.

That's what happened with the thirteen colonies. The British Parliament had hoped the laws it passed would make the colonists see how wrong they had been. They wanted the colonists to stop rebelling. They wanted them do what they were told. Instead, the American colonies stood together and grew stronger. The differences between Britain and the colonies became even greater. The colonies pulled together on the same side against the British.

A statue of a
Minuteman stands in
Boston

Chapter 2
TAKING A STAND FOR INDEPENDENCE

The colonists thought Britain should listen to them. All they wanted was someone to stand up for them in the British Parliament. They weren't asking for anything wrong or silly.

But instead, Parliament made harsher laws. Parliament tried to punish the colonists. The British Parliament thought the American colonies were out of line. It thought it needed to make the colonists obey.

At first, the colonists didn't want to break away from Britain. Most of them just wanted to find some way to work things out.

British soldiers had been sent to the colonies. This was part of the Intolerable Act. The soldiers were there to make sure the colonists obeyed the law. The colonists didn't like them being there. The colonists formed secret armies in case they needed to protect themselves from the British soldiers. These armies were called **militias**. They watched the British soldiers. They wanted to make sure they knew what the British might do.

A **militia** is a group of ordinary citizens who fight only in times of need. A militia is a group of ordinary citizens who fight only in times of need.

These groups called themselves Patriots. A patriot means someone who stands up for his or her country. The colonists who called themselves Patriots were beginning to think of America as their country. They still thought of America as a part of Britain—but they were ready to do whatever they had to do to protect their rights.

Other colonists called themselves Loyalists. These people were loyal to Britain. They didn't want to make trouble with Britain. They believed loyalty to the British king and to Parliament was more important than their rights. They thought it would be better to just pay the taxes, even if they didn't like them.

On the evening of April 18, 1775, the Patriots in Massachusetts found out that the Redcoats—the British soldiers—were about to do something. The Redcoats were going

Illustration of Paul Revere's ride

Battle at Concord's North Bridge

to Concord to destroy all the town's weapons. The British were afraid the Patriots might attack them. They wanted to make sure they couldn't.

Paul Revere, one of the Patriots, rode through the night. He told everyone what was going on. He gathered the members of the militia. The militia called themselves Minutemen. They could be ready to go in a minute.

And by morning, they were ready. Almost seventy Minutemen waited for the British. They blocked the road in Lexington. Now the Redcoats couldn't get to Concord. The British leader was frustrated. He wanted these men out of the road. But they wouldn't move. Finally, he ordered his men to attack the Minutemen.

THE SHOT HEARD 'ROUND THE WORLD

This line is from a famous poem written by the American author Ralph Waldo Emerson. A single gunshot began the war that led to the birth of the United States. That shot wasn't *really* heard around the world of course. But it did change the entire world forever. The United States has shaped world history ever since its birth. What's more, the ideas the colonists fought for—ideas about freedom and rights—spread to other countries all around the world.

The fight was over quickly. The British thought they had won. But that first shot became known as "the shot heard round the world." That shot was the beginning of the War of **Independence**. We also call it the **Revolutionary** War.

But Britain didn't know that yet. The Redcoats marched on to Concord. Nobody was waiting to attack them in Concord. The soldiers went through the town. They destroyed any weapons they found. They burned the courthouse.

From a hill near town, the Patriots watched. As the day went on, more and more Patriots arrived.

Then, late in the morning, the Patriots attacked. The Redcoats were surprised. They knew now they hadn't taken the Patriots seriously enough. All that day, Patriots and Redcoats fought between Concord and Boston. By night, it was clear that the Patriots wouldn't give up.

The fighting in Massachusetts was only the beginning of the Revolutionary War. On May 10, the Second Continental Congress met in Philadelphia. They created a Continental Army. George Washington would command it.

Meanwhile, most colonists still thought of themselves as British. Most of them weren't trying to form a separate country. They still just wanted Parliament to take them seriously.

Then, in January of 1776, a man named Thomas Paine wrote a little book called *Common Sense*. He was a Patriot who believed that America was his country, not Britain. Paine wrote that the American colonies should break away from Britain. He said that

A country with **independence** makes its own laws and decisions and doesn't need another country's support.

Something is called **revolutionary** when it makes a big change from how things were done in the past.

America was so different from Britain that it already was a different country.

People couldn't stop talking about *Common Sense*. In June, the Continental Congress decided they should write a Declaration of Independence. Thomas Jef-

George Washington addressing the troops

ferson wrote most of it. Other people helped him. On July 4, 1776, the members of Congress said they agreed with the Declaration of Independence. That date—the Fourth of July— would now always be known as Independence Day.

For the next several years, the fighting continued. Now, though, the Americans were fighting for more than their rights. Now they were fighting for their freedom. They were fighting for their own country. No longer were they just trying to make things work as part of Britain.

As the months passed, the Americans won more battles. France joined their fight against Britain. This

Thomas Paine

encouraged the Americans. It made the British angry. It also told Britain that America was here to stay.

In April 1782, the British Parliament decided to stop fighting. Slowly, the Redcoats left America. Finally, Britain agreed to accept the United States of America. It was no longer a group of British colonies. It was its own country.

But what would happen next? The Americans had won the war. Now, they had to start building a country. And that was a very big job.

Trumbull's mural of the signing of the Declaration of Independence

To all to whom

these Presents shall come, we the under signed Delegates of the States affixed to our Names send greeting. Whereas the Delegates of the United States of America in Congress assembled did on the fifteenth day of November in the Year of our Lord One Thousand Seven Hundred and Seventy seven, and in the Second Year of the Independence of America agree to certain articles of Confederation and perpetual Union between the States of New hampshire, Massachusetts bay, Rhode island and Providence Plantations, Connecticut, New York, New Jersey, Pennsylvania, Delaware, Maryland, Virginia, North Carolina, South Carolina and Georgia in the Words following, viz. "Articles of Confederation and perpetual Union between the States of New hampshire, Massachusetts bay, Rhode island and Providence Plantations, Connecticut, New York, New Jersey, Pennsylvania, Delaware, Maryland, Virginia, North Carolina, South Carolina and Georgia.

Article I. The Stile of this confederacy shall be "The United States of America."

Article II. Each state retains its sovereignty, freedom and independence, and every Power, Jurisdiction and right, which is not by this confederation expressly delegated to the United States, in Congress assembled.

Article III. The said states hereby severally enter into a firm league of friendship with each other, for their common defence, the security of their Liberties, and their mutual and general welfare, binding themselves to assist each other, against all force offered to, or attacks made upon them, or any of them, on account of religion, sovereignty, trade, or any other pretence whatever.

The Articles of Confederation

Article IV. The better to secure and perpetuate mutual friendship and intercourse among the people of the different states in this union, the

Chapter 3
CREATING A NEW COUNTRY

Fighting and winning the War of Independence felt good. Now, though, the leaders of the new country had to figure out how to govern the United States.

Back in 1776, the Continental Congress had asked Thomas Jefferson to write the Declaration of Independence. It had said that the United States would be its own country. It would no longer be part of Britain. At the same time, Congress asked another man, John Dickinson, to write the **Articles** of **Confederation**. These laid out the rules for the new country.

Dickinson was not the kind of man who liked change. He hadn't thought the colonies should separate from Britain. Once they did, he wanted the colonies—which would now be called states—to work under a strong **central** government. The central government

To **govern** is to guide and give leadership.

Articles are small statements.

A **confederation** is an agreement between a group of states to work together.

A **central** government makes decisions that affect states across the country.

would have the most control. This meant that the states would not have as much power, and that the country as a whole would have more power.

The other members of the Continental Congress did not like Dickinson's ideas. They worried about giving too much power to a central government. They were afraid that the United States might do the same things that Britain had. They did not want to lose their freedom again. That's why they wanted the states to have their own governments. They wanted to give the states most of the power. The central government would tie them together, but it would have little power. They thought the states should form a "**league** of friendship."

For months, all the while the war for independence went on, Congress argued about the Articles of Confederation. Finally, they came up with a **compromise**. They made changes to what John Dickinson had written. On November 15, 1777, they voted to accept the new Articles. Congress would act as the central government. Representatives or delegates from each state would make up Congress.

Congress still had power. It could decide when the country was going to go to war. It could make **treaties**. It could print money. Congress could make all the decisions that affected the whole country. Before Congress could make any decision, though, at least nine out of the thirteen states had to agree. If they wanted to change the Articles of Confederation, all the states had to agree.

A **league** is like a confederation, but it is a looser agreement. It doesn't force members of the group to listen to each other or work together.

When two groups believe two different things, they will sometimes make a **compromise**—they each agree to give up something and meet the other halfway.

Treaties are promises or agreements that a country makes.

Colonial currency

These ideas all seemed good to Congress at the time. They wanted to make sure nobody would be able to take their freedom away again. As soon as the war was over, though, they ran into problems.

A lot of the problems had to do with money. The war had started because of taxes. The new country decided that Congress wouldn't be allowed to collect taxes. Congress needed money to do its job, though. Each state agreed to give money to help run the country. But the states found out they didn't have enough money. They couldn't pay their own bills and still give Congress the money they had said they would.

The United States now owned the land between the original thirteen colonies and the Mississippi River. (Of course, they had taken this land from the Native people who lived there first!) Congress was in charge of this area. They decided to sell pieces of this land to people who wanted to live there. This let them raise money on their own.

Congress had decided that once the number of people in a new territory got to 5,000, it would have a governor. It would also be allowed then to send delegates to Congress. These delegates wouldn't be allowed to vote. They would be allowed to tell Congress what their territory needed, though. Once the population got to 60,000, the territory could write a state **constitution**. Then they could send their constitution to Congress. Once Congress had approved it, the territory could become a state.

New states would have all the same rights as the original states. Congress wanted to make sure no part of the country would have fewer rights than another. This was an important idea in the new United States. It was also very different from the way most countries worked.

Another problem quickly came up. The treaty that ended the war said that British companies could collect the money the original colonies had owed them. But the states didn't have enough money to pay the colonies' debts. To get the money, a lot of states started taxing their residents. People were angry about the high taxes. Some of them lost everything they owned. Some ended up in debtors' prison.

A **constitution** is a set of laws and rules that tell how a state or country should be run.

WHO OWNED AMERICA?

When the settlers from Europe arrived in North America, people were already living on the land. At first, the colonists worked out agreements with the Native people. The colonists took land they thought was empty. Most of the Native people were hunters. They weren't farmers the way the Europeans were. This meant that most of the land looked empty to the settlers. Soon more and more white people lived in the colonies. They needed more and more land. They pushed the Native people back. They fought wars with the Natives. Americans started to believe that God had given them the entire continent, from sea to sea. They thought God wanted them to live there. They felt it was right to take the land away from the Natives.

What do you think?

Colonial farmer (reenactment)

These high taxes seemed very unfair to most people. They had fought a war to get away from taxes like these!

By 1786, one group of farmers in Massachusetts had had enough. A man named Daniel Shays led them. The group kept the debtors' courts from meeting.

Like the colonists twenty years earlier, Shays and his men didn't think they were doing anything wrong. They thought the taxes were unfair. They were standing up for their rights. They thought the Massachusetts government would agree with them and lower the taxes.

This didn't happen, though. The governor, James Bowdoin, thought Shays was dangerous. He believed Shays needed to be stopped. Bowdoin and other Massachusetts leaders used their own money to hire an army to stop Shays' group.

In January 1787, Shays and a group of 2,000 men attacked the **armory** in Springfield, Massachusetts. Bowdoin had been ignoring them. Shays and his followers were really angry now. They still just wanted the government to listen to them.

Before Shays and his men got to the armory, Bowdoin's army stopped them. The army fired cannons at Shays' men. Four men were killed. Another twenty were wounded.

The farmers were shocked. They had never thought it would go this far. They scattered and ran into the woods. Shays and the other leaders of the rebellion escaped to Vermont.

The Shays Rebellion showed the Continental Congress that things weren't working. Something had to change. Congress hadn't been able to do anything to make things better in Massachusetts. They hadn't had the power to do that. Clearly, the central government needed to be stronger.

By 1787, Congress was ready to start working on a completely new Constitution.

Daniel Shays' rebellion

An **armory** is a building that houses weapons.

Chapter 4
THE CONSTITUTIONAL CONVENTION

On May 25, 1787, the Constitutional Convention began. James Madison, from Virginia, was one of the delegates. He was excited. He wanted to get started on the new constitution.

Madison and other men from his state had made the Virginia Plan. The Virginia Plan was an idea for how to make the new constitution work. It would be very different from the Articles of Confederation.

Under the Virginia Plan, the **federal** government would have power over the state governments. Madison wanted to make sure the federal government didn't have too much power, though.

All the delegates knew the federal government needed some power. The Articles of Confederation hadn't given it enough power. The Virginia Plan would make a federal government that was built in sections. This would make sure the power was split between each section. Each section would have different jobs.

The **federal** government is the central government, which is today based in Washington, D.C.

The Virginia Plan made the United States a **republic**. That meant that people would vote to elect the men who ran the country. These men would represent the people. They were called representatives.

States with more people would have more representatives. States with fewer people living in them would have fewer representatives. That seemed fair to most of the larger states. The smaller states weren't as happy, though. They worried they would have less power because of their size.

The New Jersey delegates came up with a different plan. Each state would have one vote, no matter how many people lived in the state. Now, the larger states weren't happy. They didn't like the New Jersey Plan. They didn't think it was right that small states should be counted the same way they were.

For weeks, the delegates argued. No one could agree. No one wanted to give in even a little bit.

Finally, Roger Sherman from Connecticut came up with a third idea. Sherman thought the government should have two sections. This was like the Virginia Plan. These sections would be called **legislative** houses. But Sherman's idea for these two houses was a compromise between the Virginia Plan and the New Jersey Plan. Sherman's plan said that in one house, delegates from each state would be elected based on population. In the other house, each state would have the same number of votes.

At first, nobody paid much attention to Sherman's idea. They just kept arguing.

Then Alexander Hamilton, from New York, presented still another plan. Hamilton's plan gave the states almost no power. Instead, the governor of the federal government

A **republic** is a country in which people vote for their leaders.

Legislative means having to do with making laws.

would have the most power. Also, all the representatives and the governor would be elected for life. Most of the delegates really didn't like Hamilton's ideas. They called it the British Plan. It was much too close to the way things worked in Britain. The United States wanted to do things differently.

Finally, the delegate from Maryland, Luther Martin, said he thought everyone should think more about Sherman's idea. The other delegates agreed. This was the plan they decided to go with.

The convention wasn't over yet. The delegates still disagreed on a lot of things.

One thing they disagreed about was slavery. Some thought they should end slavery immediately. Other delegates had

Alexander Hamilton

slaves. Many of them depended on slaves to run their large farms and make them money. These men didn't want to end slavery. Finally, they made another compromise. They agreed that the federal government would have the power to end slavery. But the government promised not to do that for another twenty years.

Slavery caused other arguments. Should the number of slaves in a state count when figuring out how many representatives a state should have? A state with a lot of slaves

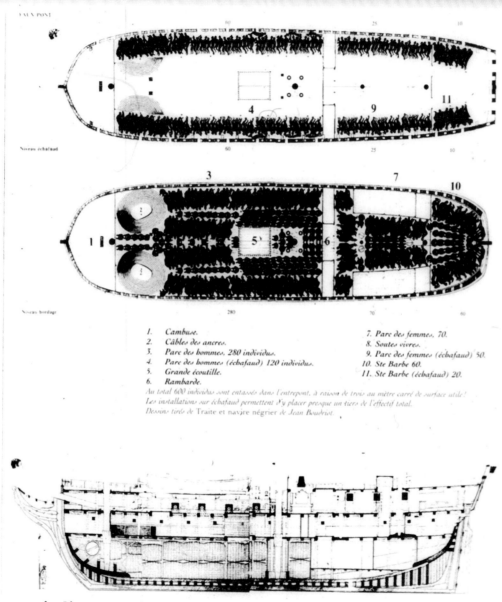

1. Cambuse.
2. Câbles des ancres.
3. Parc des hommes, 280 individus.
4. Parc des hommes (échafaud) 120 individus.
5. Grande écoutille.
6. Rambarde.
7. Parc des femmes, 70.
8. Soutes vivres.
9. Parc des femmes (échafaud) 50.
10. Ste Barbe 60.
11. Ste Barbe (échafaud) 20.

Au total 600 individus sont entassés dans l'entrepont, à raison de trois au mètre carré de surface utile!
Les installations sur échafaud permettent d'y placer presque un tiers de l'effectif total.
Dessins tirés de Traite et navire négrier de Jean Boudriot.

A diagram of a slave ship shows the cramped conditions

could get more representatives if they counted their slaves. The states with lots of slaves were in the South. Many Southern states thought they should count the slaves. This would give the South more power in the country. Most Northern states thought that wouldn't be fair. They worried the Southern states might just bring in more slaves to get

STATES RIGHTS— OR FEDERAL POWER?

Right at the beginning, Americans split into two groups—the Federalists and the Antifederalists. The Federalists liked the new Constitution. They wanted a stronger federal government. The Antifederalists, on the other hand, worried about giving the federal government too much power. They wanted to keep more power for the states. We no longer use these words (Federalist and Antifederalist), but Americans still argue over this same thing. Should states be able to make their own laws about things like same-sex marriage, the environment, and abortion? Or should the federal government be able to pass laws for the entire country? People don't agree.

What do you think?

Portrait of James Madison who went on to become the fourth president of the United States.

more representatives. The North didn't want the South having more power.

Finally, the men made another compromise. They would count each slave as three-fifths of a person.

Most of the delegates had agreed at last. They were ready now to write the new constitution. Then representatives from all the states needed to sign it.

Under the Articles of Confederation, all the states had to agree on the Constitution. Now, though, the delegates changed that rule. They said that only nine out of thirteen states had to sign it. They were afraid nothing would ever get done if they had to wait for everyone to agree! Rhode Island hadn't even sent any delegates to the Constitutional Convention.

A lot of people were upset about this change. They were afraid Congress was already trying to take away their power. They worried they might lose some of their freedom.

One by one, state representatives signed the Constitution. As more states agreed, the others felt they should go along with the rest. The last states to sign the Constitution still weren't sure it was the right thing. But they went ahead and signed it anyway. They knew it was time for America to move forward. Rhode Island was the last state to sign the Constitution. Rhode Island didn't say yes to the Constitution until three years later, on May 29, 1790.

Bill of Rights

Congress of the United States,

begun and held at the City of New York, on
Wednesday, the fourth of March, one thousand seven hundred and eighty nine.

The Conventions of a number of the States having, at the time of their adopting the Constitution, expressed a desire, in order to prevent misconstruction or abuse of its powers, that further declaratory and restrictive clauses should be added: And as extending the ground of public confidence in the Government, will best insure the beneficent ends of its institution:

Resolved, by the SENATE and HOUSE of REPRESENTATIVES of the UNITED STATES of AMERICA in Congress assembled, two thirds of both Houses concurring. That the following Articles be proposed to the Legislatures of the several States, as Amendments to the Constitution of the United States; all, or any of which articles, when ratified by three fourths of the said Legislatures, to be valid to all intents and purposes, as part of the said Constitution, viz.

Articles in addition to, and Amendment of the Constitution of the United States of America, proposed by Congress, and ratified by the Legislatures of the several States, pursuant to the fifth Article of the Original Constitution.

Article the first ...... After the first enumeration required by the first Article of the Constitution, there shall be one Representative for every thirty thousand, until the number shall amount to one hundred, after which, the proportion shall be so regulated by Congress, that there shall be not less than one hundred Representatives, nor less than one Representative for every forty thousand persons, until the number of Representatives shall amount to two hundred, after which, the proportion shall be so regulated by Congress, that there shall not be less than two hundred Representatives, nor more than one Representative for every fifty thousand persons. [Not Ratified]

Article the second .... No law, varying the compensation for the services of the Senators and Representatives, shall take effect, until an election of Representatives shall have intervened. [Not Ratified]

Article the third .... Congress shall make no law respecting an establishment of religion, or prohibiting the free exercise thereof; or abridging the freedom of speech, or of the press; or the right of the people peaceably to assemble, and to petition the Government for a redress of grievances.

James Madison also wrote some additions to the Constitution. These were called the Bill of Rights. The Bill of Rights would limit the power of the U.S. government. It said that ten special rights—like freedom of speech, for example, and newspapers' freedom to print whatever they wanted—would be protected forever. The U.S. government could never become so strong that it could take away these rights. This was another compromise. It was a way to make everybody happy.

With the new Constitution, the United States had taken another important step as a country. Now, they needed to find the right leader.

Chapter Five
THE NEW GOVERNMENT

After the Revolutionary War, George Washington just wanted to go home. He had served as a general in the war. He had led the army. He had helped win the war. Now, he wanted a life of peace. He wanted to relax in his own home. He wanted to work on his farm in Mount Vernon, Virginia. He wanted to spend time with his wife, Martha.

Washington cared about what was going on in the new country, though. He had been chosen as one of the delegates from Virginia. Most people in the United States looked up to Washington. They thought he had done a good job leading the troops during the war. On the first day of the convention, the other delegates picked him to be the convention president.

When the convention was over, Congress set the date for the first presidential election. It would take place on February 4, 1789. For the first time, people living in America would vote for the leader of their new country.

When the votes were counted, George Washington had been elected as the first president of the United States. Everyone voted for Washington! Not a single person voted for anyone else.

Washington didn't really want to be president. He would have been much happier to stay home. He didn't think he knew enough to be president, either. Still, he wanted to do the right thing. His country had asked him to do a job. He didn't want to let his country down. So on April 30, 1789, Washington was made president of the United States. John Adams was the vice president.

Washington wanted to make sure he had good men to help him make wise decisions. He wanted people who would give him good advice. He picked men to help him run the country. Thomas Jefferson would be Secretary of State. This meant he would help the United States get along with other countries. Alexander Hamilton would be Secretary of the Treasury. He would help Washington make decisions about the country's money. Washington also chose a Secretary of War to help make decisions about the country's army. An Attorney General would help make decisions about the law.

Washington had to deal with problems right away. A big problem was the money the United States still owed Britain. Alexander Hamilton wanted to make a national bank. The national bank would take all the debts each state owed and put them together. The federal government would then be responsible for paying the whole thing. The states would give money to the national bank to help pay.

Hamilton thought a national bank would tie the states together more. He thought having them help pay each other's debts would be good for them. The Northern states thought this was a good idea. They had more debt. A national bank meant they would have help paying that debt. The Southern states disagreed. They had more money and less debt. They didn't want to help the Northern states with their debt.

Washington wasn't sure what was the right answer. He wanted to do what was best. He asked his advisors what they thought. People couldn't agree. Thomas Jefferson, especially, thought a national bank was a bad idea. He thought the Constitution didn't give the federal government the power to make a bank.

Eventually, Washington made up his mind. He decided to go with Hamilton's idea.

The argument went on, though. People all over the country took one side or the other. Washington didn't like the disagreements. He was afraid the arguments would make the country weaker.

Political parties took shape around this argument. Those who agreed with Thomas Jefferson that the bank was a bad idea became the Democratic-Republicans. Those who agreed with Hamilton became the Federalists.

Once the national bank had been created, the government had to raise money to pay the debt. Hamilton wanted to charge a tax on whiskey to get money.

In western Pennsylvania, small farmers were upset by the whiskey tax. They made a lot of whiskey. Some farmers even used whiskey instead of money. The richer people in the East didn't use whiskey much. The tax didn't bother them. That didn't seem right to

Political parties are groups of people who believe in the same basic ideas of how government should be run.

the farmers in Pennsylvania. They thought the tax was unfair, since they used whiskey so much more than people in other parts of the country did.

For a long time, the farmers tried to get out of paying the tax. They said they would obey the laws of Pennsylvania—but they didn't want to obey the laws of the United States.

In July 1784, this disagreement turned into a revolt. A mob broke into the house of the man who was in charge of the tax collectors. One of the rebels was shot and killed. Everyone got angrier. The next day, the rebels came back and burned down the house.

Washington knew he had to do something to end the rebellion. He traveled to Pennsylvania and led an army to deal with the situation. The army captured the leaders of the rebellion. The rest gave up.

People liked the way Washington handled the Whiskey Rebellion. They liked that he had taken charge of the situation. Even people who didn't like the whiskey tax felt good about President Washington. They liked that he had gone to Pennsylvania himself. Washington's action helped people accept the stronger federal government.

The United States also had to deal with problems from outside the country. First George Washington, and then John Adams, the second president, had to take care of trouble with Britain and France. Both presidents sent men to Europe to talk with the British and French. These men were able to find ways to settle the problems. By 1800, these problems had mostly disappeared. The rest of the world was starting to respect the United States.

The first years after the Revolutionary War had brought many changes for the United States. The country had grown up a lot. It had written a constitution. It had elected leaders. It had taken care of problems that had come up. It had proven to the world that America was here to stay!

POLITICAL PARTIES

Washington was afraid political parties would tear the country apart. But they actually made it stronger. Having different political parties let people have more control over what their leaders did. The two main parties balanced each other. If one party started making a lot of bad decisions, people could change things by voting for the other party. Neither party could be too powerful.

Today the main political parties in the United States are the Republicans and the Democrats. The Republicans are most like the Democratic-Republicans of George Washington's day. Republicans want the federal government to be smaller. They believe that the federal government should not get in the way of businesses. They are in favor of states' rights. Democrats are more like the Federalists. They think the federal government should be stronger. They believe the federal government should take charge of all the problems the country faces.

Why do you think it makes the United States stronger to have two political parties? Do you think it could ever make the country less strong? Why or why not?

FIND OUT MORE

In Books

Martin, Joseph Plumb. *A Narrative of a Revolutionary Soldier*. New York: Signet Classics, 2001.

Murray, Stuart. *American Revolution*. New York: DK Publishing, 2002.

Nardo, Don. *The American Revolution*. San Diego, Calif.: KidHaven Press, 2002.

Rappaport, Doreen and Joan Vergniero. *Victory or Death: Stories of the American Revolution*. New York: HarperCollins, 2003.

Stewart, Gail B. *Life of a Soldier.* San Diego, Calif.: Lucent Books, 2003.

On the Internet

Boston Massacre
www.bostonmassacre.net

Continental Congress and Constitutional Convention
memory.loc.gov/ammem/collections/continental

Paul Revere
www.paulreverehouse.org

Revolutionary War
americanrevwar.homestead.com

Valley Forge
www.ushistory.org/valleyforge

INDEX

ABOUT THE AUTHOR
AND THE CONSULTANT

Constance Sharp studied history and literature in college. She enjoys teaching children about the history of their world.

Dr. Jack N. Rakove is a professor of history and American studies at Stanford University, where he is director of American studies. The winner of the 1997 Pulitzer Prize in history, Dr. Rakove is the author of *The Unfinished Election of 2000*, *Constitutional Culture and Democratic Rule*, and *James Madison and the Creation of the American Republic*. He is also the president of the Society for the History of the Early American Republic.

PICTURE CREDITS
Photoshop.com: pp. 20, 30
U.S. Library of Congress: p. 32

To the best knowledge of the publisher, all other images are in the public domain. If any image has been inadvertently uncredited, please notify Harding House Publishing Services, Vestal, New York 13850, so that rectification can be made for future printings.